Plants, Animals, and People Live Together

Elliot Paderewski

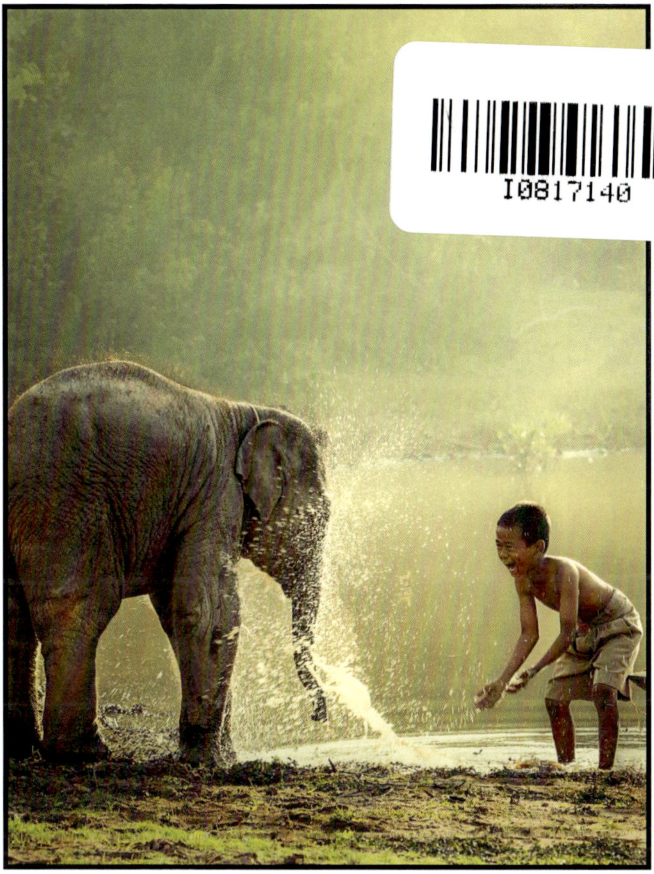

New York

People, animals,
and plants live together.

They help each other
live and grow.

Animals help plants.
They spread seeds.

They help spread pollen, too.

Animals need to eat plants.
People need plants, too.

Plants give animals and people energy.

Words to Know

animals

people

plants

pollen

seeds